Selected Poems

COLETTE BRYCE was born in Derry in 1970.
After studying in England, she settled in London for
some years where she received an Eric Gregory Award in
1995 and won the National Poetry Competition in 2003.
She has published four poetry collections with Picador,
most recently *The Whole & Rain-domed Universe* (2014),
recipient of a Christopher Ewart-Biggs Award in memory of
Seamus Heaney. She has held literary fellowships at various
universities in the UK, Ireland and the US, and currently
lives in Newcastle upon Tyne where she works as
a freelance writer and editor. She received a
Cholmondeley Award for poetry in 2010.

Colette Bryce

Selected Poems

PICADOR

First published 2017 by Picador
an imprint of Pan Macmillan
20 New Wharf Road, London N1 9RR
Associated companies throughout the world
www.panmacmillan.com

ISBN 978-1-5098-4038-0

1 3 5 7 9 8 6 4 2

A CIP catalogue record for this book is available from the British Library.

Printed and bound by CPI Group (UK) Ltd, Croydon, CR0 4YY

Contents

Selected Poems

Line,

you were drawn in the voice of my mother;
not past Breslin's, don't step over.
Saturday border, breach in the slabs,
creep to the right, Line,
sidelong, crab,

cut up the tarmac, sunder the flowers,
drop like an anchor,
land in The Moor as a stringball
ravelling under the traffic,
up, you're the guttering scaling McCafferty's,

maze through the slating,
dive from sight and down into history, Line,
take flight in the chase of the fences,
leap the streets
where lines will meet you, race you, lead

you into the criss-crossed heart of the city
of lines for the glory, lines for the pity.

Break

Soldier boy, dark and tall, sat for a rest
on Crumlish's wall. *Come on over.*

Look at my Miraculous Medal.
Let me punch your bulletproof vest. *Go on, try.*

The gun on your knees is blackened metal.
Here's the place where the bullets sleep.

Here's the catch and here's the trigger.
Let me look through the eye.

Soldier, you sent me for cigs but a woman
came back and threw the money in your face.

I watched you backtrack, alter, cover
your range of vision, shoulder to shoulder.

Itch

I believe that Jesus lives
deep in the ditch of my mother's ear,

an unreachable itch that never leaves.
And I believe when Jesus breathes

a million microscopic hairs
lean in the breeze like sapling trees.

Things I begin to tell her,
I believe sometimes she cannot hear

for the whispering like wishes
of Jesus softly breathing there.

Lines

for PB

I have given birth to a see-through child.
In the midwife's cloth its skin cools
and sets to a delicate shell, not quite
opaque but vague like frosted glass.

Closer, I see the insides press
like noses smudged on windows,
and a web of a million arteries
bleached with a terrible absence of blood.

I don't know what to do with it.
I am trying to get back to my mother.
But the cab driver drops it as I try to pay
and all I can do is stand here and stare

at my broken baby, spilt across the kerb —
when my sister springs from a hopscotch game,
skipping towards me, laughing. Calm down,
she says, It all fits back together, look. See?

The Pieces

Transit van, fireguard, canvas,
standard lamp, a wintered lake,
art room, lips, a baby bath,
two hands, a knife, a wedding cake,

pavement, sandals, banister,
champagne, rucksack, bus stop, ear,
sunset, ceiling, knee sock, corner,
forehead, skyline, sofa, car,

Santa Claus, cartoon, carnations,
Easter egg, Communion veil,
ocean, windows, LPs, onions,
waving painted fingernails,

breast, a mattress, transit van,
witch's cat, a threshold, ash,
eyebrow, paintbrush, bed sheet, snow-man,
foot, balloon, a black moustache,

forearm, ribbons, dinner plates,
turpentine, baptismal font,
cashpoint, paper party hats,
pumpkin, yellow plastic phone,

ambulance, red-brick houses,
pinafore, the Isle of Skye,
sand, a priest, a pair of glasses,
swimsuit, tinsel, altar, thigh.

Phone

Though we've come to hate this line
we call; stuck evenings when we've dried
the well of talk, we bide the time
in small long-distance silences
and lend ourselves as audience
to voices washed from tense to tense
across the middle air.

So, often, more than I can bear,
missing you brings this desire
at least to hear and to be heard
and then, there's something to be said
for this. For this becomes a web,
becomes a hair, a strength, a thread,
a tightrope between us, in all fairness,
you in my hereness, me in your thereness.

Woman & Turkey

I needed a drink before handling it,
the clammy skin, thin and raw.
I remembered touching a dead bishop once;
Sign of the Cross, shivers.

Its feet, ditched in the sink, reached
like withered hands appealing.
The crack of its bones chilled my own.
I sank another, severed the neck.

The membranous eyes were unsettling,
the shrunken head bereft on the block,
the clutch and the squelch as innards slopped out –
gizzard, heart, lungs.

I finished the bottle to see it through
and caught the scene in the night behind glass,
a corpse like a glove to my wrist.
I am sick to the stomach of Christmas.

It's hazy then until Boxing Day,
a shock of light across the room.
I wake to blood trapped under my nails,
to the delicate snap of a wishbone.

Form

For some time I have been starving myself,
and not in the interest of fashion,
but because it is something to do
and I do it well.

I'm writing this as my only witness
has been the glass on the wall.
Someone must know what I've done
and there's no one to tell.

Commitment is the main thing. After this,
the emptiness, the hunger isn't a sacrifice
but a tool. I found I was gifted, good.
And full of my vocation, sat or stood

at the mirror just watching my work
take shape, conform to my critical eye.
Or would lie, supine, stomach shrinking,
contracting, perfecting its concave line.

Each day gave a little more: depth to the shallows
of the temples, definition to the cheek,
contrast to the clavicle, the ankle bone, the rib,
the raised X-ray perception of my feet.

But one night I dressed and went for a walk
and felt a latent contamination of eyes
from windows and cars. I'd been feeling
strange, somehow encased, the hollow rush

of my own breath like tides in the shell
of my own head. A woman passed
and I saw myself in her glance,
her expression blank as a future.

The next day I woke to double vision,
everything suddenly terribly clear, only twinned.
My hearing, too, was distracted.
I sipped some water and retched.

My speech, when I test it, has stretched
to a distant slur like a voice from behind a door.
I would think I was losing my mind
if it wasn't behind all this from the start.

Tonight there's an almost imperceptible buzzing
in my bones, like the sound of electric razors,
a lawn-mower several gardens down.
I worry that they're crumbling

under my skin, dissolving like aspirin.
I worry that my bones are caving in.
When I sit my joints begin to set.
I try to stand and I'm hit by a shift in gravity,

the point where an aircraft lifts and enters flight.
And I think my sight is burning out.
I think it is losing its pupil heart.
Objects are calmly vacating their outlines,

colours slowly absorbing the dark.
In my dream the shovels uncover a hare,
preserved in its form, its self-shaped lair,
and I'm travelling in. There is no going back.

Wine

The corkscrew lifts its elegant arms
like the Pope greeting tourists
on his balcony. Tonight we drink

religiously, fill to a shivering inch
of the brink, carefully, almost
warily. Tonight I drink to you,

and you to me, but this time,
seriously; as if following, word
for word in the clink, a ceremony.

Young

Loose stacks of cassettes collapse
to the slam of the door behind us.
We take the stairs
in twos and threes,

we don't know where we might be
this time next year,
but meanwhile,
we apply to the future in lunch-breaks;

taste the possibility, the sweet adhesive
strip of A4 envelopes on tongues,
punch the day and run
to post, to home, and out.

We eye each other up as future lovers;
our faces smooth as blank maps
of undiscovered countries,
where only we might go.

We mean to go, we thumb the guides,
we spin the globe and halt it
at Calcutta, then Alaska, now Japan,
and plan. Imagine.

Not for us the paper lanterns of remember,
but the hard bright bulbs of sheer want.
We reminisce at length
about the future, which is better;

we harbour it in our hearts
like a terrible crush. We laugh
and drink to this in rented rooms.
We think Not this, but older, elsewhere, soon.

Plot Summary, Scene 4

Then, I would meet you again
and would greet you in fifteen different languages,
like the Pope;
approach you in a cool embrace and kiss
alternate zones of your face, solemnly, like a delegate
from some forgotten independent state
whose population waits, has staked on this
all hope.

I would talk like the rattle of chairs
across a monumental marble hall
where throngs have all stood up to toast your cause.
I would lead the applause.
And we would sign on the dotted line
come nightfall. And together,
turn and smile for the blinding flashbulbs.

Wish You Were

Here, an aftertaste of traffic taints
the city's breath, as mornings
yawn and bare this street

like teeth. Here, airplanes leaving
Heathrow scare this house
to trembling; these rooms protect

their space with outstretched walls,
and wait. And evenings fall
like discs in a jukebox, playing

a song called *Here,* night after night.
Wish you were. Your postcards
land in my hall like meteorites.

Griffon

We queue at the valley's screened enclosure,
take our places, pay a price, a scatter of coins
apiece for this; for you, a mash of blood and flesh,
a metal pail, a tethered foot, a note on natural habitat,
a roaring anger in your gut that keeps you lunging
from your rope, upward, to your element.

A whistle shrieks

and you release your vast scaffolding of wings,
perform a weighted, awkward flight, a single beat
from A to B, then low across our cowered heads
to A. You earn your piece of meat, regard us
with an ancient eye. Up there, a pencilled sketch
of peaks, eternity of sky, a far cry.

Cabo de São Vicente

Today, we will walk to the end of the world.
We kiss, and start the distance —
three days rested in a gale-stripped village,
one drink taken at the Last Chance Saloon.
Loves of our lives, we are blessed, convinced.
We have water and food, a known significance.

But who is this woman, rucksack-laden,
just up ahead, or tripping our heels,
stumbling on rocks in her flip-flop sandals,
sorry to bother us, wanting a match,
traipsing the cut of the sand-soft cliff,
wrestling a map in the high, high wind?

Nevers

Passions never spoken,
never broken but preserved,
never layered under marriages
or burnt to dust by fast affairs
are saints to us,

the sacred ones,
bodily enshrined
to lie in state like Bernadette
at Nevers of the mind;
amazing, garlanded and fair.

Older, at the inkling
of an accent or a smile,
we travel there.

Stones

after Stephen Spender

We kept ourselves from children who were rich,
who were shaped in the folds of newest clothes,
who were strapped in the backs of foreign cars
whose quick electric windows rose
effortlessly, that poured into the stream of traffic;

but stared, fascinated, at their orthodontic
iron smiles, their nerve-averted eyes.

They were quiet. They feared rain. They were taught
to recite in yellow rooms *Colette, Suzette,*
Jo-jo and Lou are coming here for tea...
or to sing at the prompt of a tuning fork
How merry your life must be...

They had no idea, but disappeared
to the south of France twice a year –
as we ran the streets, the lanes and squares,
a band of outlaws, ne'er-do-wells
– then left for schools we didn't know.

From walls we saw them come and go.
War-daubed faces, feathers in our hair, wild,

we never smiled.

Last Night's Fires

The street-lamp by the gutted bus
soft-ticks, watches us from the stuck
joint of its neck. There's windscreen
shattered on the ground like jewels,
diamonds, amethysts, on the school
walk. Bull Park; a wire mesh
and gravel pitch, some busted swings
bound tight about the bars.

Cars start, cough breath, raise
the lights of their eyes. A milk van,
faintly ringing. Then the fuel truck
with its damp sacks of slack
burdened on the deck; its skinny
truant rider; his cigarette, an ember.

Satellite

For all we see of you these days,
you might be living in outer space!
shouted my mother,
after my father, table cleared
of dinner plates, had poured a sea
of silver and coppers, metalfalls
from the money-drawer of the pub
where he'd spent the night before
pulling pints for the late drinkers.

We, his band of little helpers,
counted them into cityscapes
of stacks and towers – hours of fun –
our hands would turn an alien green
as, through the wall, their arguing
went on, my father circling,
there's nothing left
in this doom town for us;
my mother stood her ground.

Part of the task was to separate
the rogue harps and leaping fish
from the Queen's heads, the odd button;
even an errant dime or quarter
that had found its way across the water
bearing, on the backward swell
of the great Atlantic wishing-well,
via the till of the Telstar Bar,
news of Brooklyn, or Manhattan.

And They Call It Lovely Derry

And so, strangely enough, to Florida.
Twenty from our side of the River
Foyle and twenty more from the other,
lifted out of a 'war-torn community'
to mix three weeks in a normal society.
That was the general idea.

When we arrived we were paired
and placed with a host couple, good
church people, settled and stable.
She was the first Prod I had ever met;
a small girl, pale and introvert, who wept
for home, then sniffed, and smiled.

The husband sat at the head of the table
holding forth, hot and bothered.
He couldn't decide on the right word,
hmmed and hawed between Blacks and Coloured,
whatever, his point? They were bone idle,
wouldn't accept the jobs they were offered.

The woman dreamed of having a child.
I took to the role of living doll
and would tolerate each morning's session
under the tug of curling tongs.
I had never even heard of Racism.
We gave a concert on the last night,

forty of us, rigid with stage fright.
My whistle shrieked on a high note.
We harmonized on all the songs
but fell apart with the grand finale,
the well-rehearsed 'O I know a wee spot...'
as the group split between London and Lovely.

Device

Some express themselves like this:
circuit kit; 4 double-A batteries, 1 9-volt,
1 SPDT mini-relay, 1 M-80
rocket engine, a solar ignitor,
a pair of contacts, 1 connector; wired,
coiled and crafted together, care
taken over positives and negatives.

Dawn or before, the artist's hour,
it is placed, delicately as a gift,
under a car in a street that will flare
to a gallery in the memory,
cordoned off and spotlit for eternity.

1981

A makeshift notice in the square
says it with numbers, each day higher.
North of here, in a maze of cells,
a man cowers, says it with hunger,
skin, bone, wrought to a bare
statement. Waiting, there are others.

Days give on to days; we stall
in twos and threes in the town centre,
talk it over, say it with anger,
What's the news? It's no better.
Headlines on the evening paper
spell it out in huge letters.

Over graves and funeral cars
the vast bays of colour say it
with flowers, flowers everywhere;
heads are bowed, as mute as theirs,
that will find a voice in the darker hours,
say it with stones, say it with fire.

The Smoke

The soul of the house was the one back room
to which his life had since retreated.

The soul of the room was the TV screen
that cast its blue and yellow light

that seemed when viewed from out in the night
like something close to flame.

My father sat alone, pipe
propped at an angle to inhale:

when smoke expelled – a dragon smile,
its smell of turf or heather fires,

the room about him stretched for miles.
It was slow dismantled, tipped and spilled

and tapped to empty, thumbed bowl full,
attended to by small soul tools:

a blade, a spike, wires for the stem,
a tamping weight, a dipping flame.

The Deposition

Look how the faithful struggle with the body,
fumble for a pulse, all fingers and thumbs:
the cue balls of the eyes roll upward
in the skull; the skin glistens and stinks.
They are straightening the clothing
out of some sense of decency. Two of them
shoulder it, awkward, to the stairs,
a cruciform; the head lolling, jaw
faltering open on its hinge.
The feet trail, leave behind a slipper.
Staggering under its startling weight
of inanimate meat and bone under gravity,
they make it to the doorway, bed, deposit me,
leave me alone. They are true believers.
I am their mother. They trust me to rise
and find my way back, lie down in the body,
wake to inhabit another of my lives.

The Full Indian Rope Trick

There was no secret
murmured down through a long line
of elect; no dark fakir, no flutter
of notes from a pipe,
no proof, no footage of it –
but I did it,

Guildhall Square, noon,
in front of everyone.
There were walls, bells, passers-by;
a rope, thrown, caught by the sky
and me, young, up and away,
goodbye.

Goodbye, goodbye.
Thin air. First try.
A crowd hushed, squinting eyes
at a full sun. There
on the stones
the slack weight of a rope

coiled in a crate, a braid
eighteen summers long,
and me –
I'm long gone,
my one-off trick
unique, unequalled since.

And what would I tell them
given the chance?
It was painful; it took years.
I'm my own witness,
guardian of the fact
that I'm still here.

Pillar Talk

That magician
who stationed himself on a pillar

over Manhattan
for thirty-five hours

knows nothing whatever
of loneliness,

or how it is
for people like us

who have no soft acre
of cardboard boxes

not even the eggshell
flashbulbs of the press

or the well-meant antics
of neighbours with a mattress

to temper the thought
of the hard, hard earth,

to break the fall.
Nothing at all.

Early Version

Our boat was slow to reach Bethsaida; winds oppressed us,
fast and cold, our hands were blistered from the oars.
We'd done to death our songs and jokes, with miles
to go, when Jesus spoke:

he said he'd crouched upon the shore, alone, engaged
in silent prayer, when, looking down, he started –
saw his own image crouching there. And when he leant
and dipped his hand

he swore he felt the fingers touch, and as he rose
the image stood and, slowly, each put out a foot
and took a step, and where they met, the weight of one
annulled the other;

then how he'd moved across the lake, walked on the soles
of his liquid self, and he described how cool it felt
on his aching, dusty feet; the way he'd strode a steady
course to board the boat

where we now sat – mesmerised. He gestured out
towards the shore, along the lake, then to himself,
and asked us all to visualise, to open what he always
called our 'fettered minds'.

The Word

He arrived, confused, in groups at the harbours,
walking unsteadily over the gangways;
turned up at airports, lost in the corridors,
shunted and shoved from Control to Security;
fell, blinking and bent, a live cargo
spilled from the darks of our lorries,
dirty-looking, disarranged, full of lies, lies,
full of wild stories – threats and guns and foreign wars;
or He simply appeared, as out of the ground,
as man, woman, infant, child, darkening doorways,
tugging at sleeves with *Lady, Mister, please, please...*

There were incidents; He would ask for it –
His broken English, guttural; swaying
His way through rush hour trains, touching people,
causing trouble; peddling guilt in the market place,
His thousand hands demanding change, flocking
in rags to the steps of the church, milking
the faithful, blocking the porch, He was chased –
but arrived in greater numbers, needs misspelt
on scraps of paper, hungry, pushy, shifty, gypsy,
not comprehending *No* for an answer. What could we do?
We turned to the Word; called to our journalists, they heard

and hammered a word through the palms of His hands: SCAM.
They battered a word through the bones of His feet: CHEAT.
Blood from a bogus crown trickled down,
ran into His eyes and His mouth and His throat,
OUT: He gagged, but wouldn't leave.
We rounded Him up with riot police,
drove Him in vanloads out of our streets,
away from our cities, into the tomb
and left Him there, a job well done.
We are safer now, for much has changed,
now the Word is the law is a huge, immovable stone,

should He rise again.

Fabio's Miracle

The child saw it first, tripped screaming
from the alcove, grazed her knees.
I fell to mine and prayed to God,
La Madonnina wept. I ran for the priest.

They have come to expect the blood of a beast,
plastic arteries into the eyes, hidden
crimson cavities in the porous plaster, hairline
fractures loosening to a severed head,

a chip to the glaze of a lower lid
with the tip of a blade or the point of a pin,
dye applied like a girl's cosmetics,
streaked in the blaze of a midday sun,

but tests have been done: it is real blood.
Added to this, it is male blood.
The blood of the virgin ought to be female, no?
The blood of the risen Christ or the humble Fabio?

—the city men. They come and call me
charlatan. They say I've led the poor astray.
This woman, she was cured today.
That sound you hear, is that real prayer?

It's simple. We had nothing here
and prayed for bread. Now look around.
Let *them* survive on mountain air
and I'll say *It's a miracle!*

There are guards at the gate of our little chapel,
two brass keys to the small glass case,
one for the lawyer, one for the priest,
and no more answers, no more tests.

And since? I've visited just once. The queue
of pilgrims snaked for miles. I knelt and raised
my eyes to meet her raw, clawed face,
her livid gaze. One of us smiled.

Gallery

She showed me the red earth
breaking under lightning, lightning
or else a great tear in the sky,
and I covered my eyes.
She played for me the small sounds
of white flame trembling,
the murmur of shadows
slanting from a roof, but I deafened
to her, and still wouldn't look.

When she took me
into the room of cloud
I closed the doors of my coat
around me, but she touched my arm
and she leaned to me, and put her mouth
to my mouth, lightly. There were
slate blue waves and nine ships
tilting where she left me, weighed
in the balance, wanting.

Tense

Like dry ice on a dance floor, the mist
pours over the river, ghost-
advances onto the land, over the walls
and darkened lawns, pressured
gently at the glass. Restless
in our separate beds, with only a mile
of mist between us, do we recall

or anticipate this; the first impulse,
chance opening, where one of us
will risk everything, leaned
and meets the other's lips, our mouths
fusing, hands unfastening clothes,
uncovering shoulders, breasts, burned
deeper and deeper in the kiss.

And was it you or I who will rise, later,
throw the windows wide, and let
the mist, persistent all the while,
fill the room where we lie
streamed in each other, breath in breath,
settled itself unbearably soft
on our nakedness in the moments after.

The Negatives

I know I was there. I'm sure of it.
Or could I have imagined a day so fully?
I didn't leave early, when Lottie and Sylvie
had enough and called a cab from the village,

though I might have. I had an uneasy feeling
even then. I trusted the camera to the men,
I remember that, and the heat, the lake,
undressing; slipping the silk from my skin,

the soft water, clinging like silk
to our limbs, its lit, concentric rings.
Where have I gone? I search the prints.
There's Tom, arranging his suit on the grass

just so; as always, fastidious.
I tried one of Robert's black cigarettes
and coughed, then laughed, *cheroooots*,
he drawled, the word itself, delicious.

They are all there. The swans, fierce
by the broken cottage; William, enthralled.
Samuel, holding that stone that looked
like a skull, poor Yorick. The brimming well

where our coins fell, cut through the water,
sank in the mud into old tender.
I grip my wrist. Yes, it is real
with its ghost pulse, its pale blue rivers.

The chemist shrugged. He's an honest man.
I go back to the negatives, surely somewhere?
raise them up to the future, bright
in the trinity of the long bay windows,

think of the film, coiled safe
in its vacuum case for all these years,
my image fading like frost, my face
a pattern vanishing on glass.

You begin, of course, to doubt yourself.
And now, there is only my word for it.
And who ever listens to an old woman
with the world still spinning so fast?

Lithium

In the photograph, you could be anybody
making the most of a bright bank holiday.
We could belong to any of those parked cars.

The children, netting for life at the edge
of the stillest, silver lake,
they could be ours.

What's the matter with us?

Only a tremor in the hand.
It rained, remember, after that, a rain
we couldn't see or feel but noticed,

dipping circles on the lake
as if it existed only in reflection,
as if inverse, beneath the surface tension.

Words and Music

She moves about in the tiny flat
with the long strides of a goddess,
fixing this, or watering that,
mixing the books up, wearing my shirt.

She dials the little radio
through crashing waves of static,
through 'words, words, words!'
and finds a hidden symphony

then moves a chair to occupy
the single square of morning sun,
basks in the full length of herself,
ankles hooked on the window sill,

feet conducting sky. She asks me
if I love her. I wouldn't quite
go that far. It's just that
if she leaves me, I'm done for.

The Pines

All around,
the tapering pines
teeter, teeter,
jittery,
and with good cause
on a ground crossed
and counter-crossed
with the fallen,
that seem to sink,
are slowly lost
to a lush mess
of grasses, mosses.

Each is born
to bow and die
but one will tilt,
from time to time,
awkwardly
to another's arms
and, through the dark,
a met tension
seeks out
its release in sound.

Lovers
and insomniacs,
keepers
of the secret hours,
lift your heads
and listen, listen;
some will know
the low glissando
worked on the fretboard
of the night; some,
the call of one
speared soul
under a fearful,
startling moonlight.

+

Through the cabin window's haze
we watch the black shadow of our plane
free itself from the undercarriage,
separate, then fall away.

With it falls the sunlit runway,
grids of crops and reservoirs, then all
the scattered glitter of a city
falls, the tattered coastline of a country

plunges out of view.
And just when you might expect to see
the globe in brilliant clarity,
cloud fills the tiny screen

and we, who haven't taken off
at all, wait, seatbelts on,
for the world to turn and return to us
as it always does, sooner or later,

to fix itself to the craft again
at a point marked with the shadow of a plane,
pencilled now on a runway, growing
larger under Irish rain.

from *The Observations of Aleksandr Svetlov*

An Old Woman

I realised, mending your precious atlas,
how many things I would love to tell you;
rubbish we used to impart to each other
that nobody else would be interested in.
I'd like your opinion on the new neighbour.
His manner, I think, has a sinister edge, and you
could interpret a face, the most accurate map.

Imagine your pique if I didn't inform you
that Ivan, the postmaster, burgled himself
for his gambling debts (he got six years)
but his wife, Rozita, weathered the storm
and established a rather attractive little shop
of cheeses and rustic fare from the villages.
Remember Rozita? Cousin of Igor and Yuz?

In all the designs we'd invent of our lives
I would die first, so you could have peace
to put our affairs and the house in order.
Look at me now, gluing the atlas,
wearing your apron like an old woman,
an old woman with a mind still tuned
to the sorts of things you'd be interested in.

from *The Observations of Aleksandr Svetlov*

So Much

People flee this town more and more.
No longer thrilled by the blurry lights
of Moscow, they take to the sky and drop
like seeds all over this fertile earth.
I don't know how they can live as foreigners,
bowing and scraping to the Americans. What
about their history? What happens to their families?
What damage to our language as they twist
their mouths around the implausible sounds?

Here, when you haven't the heart for words,
when silence sits like a stone in your soul,
the slightest look or gesture is as good,
so much is already understood.

In Defence of Old Men Dozing in Bookshops

There are days I drop in on Mikhail at the shop
when time will diminish like flour tap-tapped
through a sieve. I position myself at the window
and open a volume, selected at random
but normally fiction (for the window seat
is very well placed for the longest lies).
Having polished my glasses, I then proceed
to read and absorb the opening sentence.
For example: *During a small-bow contest*
one of the archers coughs. Isn't that odd?
I turn it over, open again, and feast my eyes

on the termination: *'It is premature*
to speak of Autumn', she replied,
'yet I feel myself ascending
nine times towards you in the night'.
Now what would you make of that?
Indeed. So consider that old 'has-been'
who seems to be dozing in a spot of sun;
he may be, in truth, in the act of applying
the logic derived from a lifetime of dying
to the problem of what could have possibly happened
in between.

A Spider

I trapped a spider in a glass,
a fine-blown wineglass.
It shut around him, silently.
He stood still, a small wheel
of intricate suspension, cap
at the hub of his eight spokes,
inked eyes on stalks; alert,
sensing a difference.
I meant to let him go
but still he taps against the glass
all Marcel Marceau
in *the wall that is there but not there*,
a circumstance I know.

When I Land in Northern Ireland

When I land in Northern Ireland I long for cigarettes,
for the blue plume of smoke hitting the lung with a thud and, God,
the quickening blood as the stream administers the nicotine.
Stratus shadows darkening the crops
when coming in to land,
coming in to land.

What's your poison?
A question in a bar
draws me down through a tunnel of years
to a time preserved in a cube of fumes, the seventies-yellowing
walls of remembrance; everyone smokes and talks about the land,
the talk about the land, our spoiled inheritance.

The Harm

On the walk to school you have stopped
at the one significant lamppost, just to be sure
(if you're late where's the harm?),
and are tracing the cut of the maker's name in raised print
and yes, you are certain it is still ticking,
softly ticking where it stands on the corner

opposite McCaul's corner-
shop. Not that you had expected it to stop.
At worst, all you'll get from the teacher is a good ticking
off. When it goes off, and you are sure
it will be soon, this metal panel with its neat square print
will buckle like the lid of Pandora's tin and harm

will blow from the mechanical heart, harm
in a wild cacophony of colour. A car takes the corner
as you start to cross and the driver's face imprints
itself on your mind forever, a whitened mask, as he stops
a hair's breadth from the sure
and quickened ticking

of your child's heart — a little clock or timer ticking.
'For God's sake stay on the pavement out of harm's
way!' the woman who grabs you says. 'Sure
haven't you been told how to cross a road? This corner
has already seen the death of my daughter. Stop
and look, and look both ways!' She prints

her grip on your thin bare arm, the sour imprint
of alcohol on her too-close breath. Then the ticking
of a wheel, as a man on a bicycle slows to a stop,
dismounts, and tells her 'It's okay Mary, there's no harm
done.' He leads her from the corner,
talking in her ear, 'It's alright Mary. Yes, yes, I am sure.'

He motions with his eyes for you to leave but, unsure,
you wait, frozen by the lamppost, the lettering print-
ing ridges in your palm, until you run at last to the opposite corner
and walk to the school, the woman's words still ticking
in your head, her notion of harm
and the thought of her daughter, unable to stop

missing school. You are sure, as sure as the ticking
lamppost is a bomb, its timer on, of harm, printed
forever on the corner where the woman's world has stopped.

Volcanoes

The fine, wrought-iron furniture
is adult-sized yet somehow miniature,
painted a pine or a racing green;
and our hostess could be the new Monroe
wearing the face from a framed-up poster
hung in the lab of my science teacher
all those lives ago
who would clamp her palm like a gag on the smile
to show us the anger in the eyes.

Next to the murmuring guests, a child
is lying, stretched out on the lawn,
for the child has learned of the curvature
of the earth and is listening for the core,
the core that sounds like an old gas fire,
quiet, yet persistent, *there*,
the roar of isolated flame —
impossible — then a mind ablaze,
a mind ablaze with a deep unease.

The earth has vents, I tell the child,
vents release and vents restrain.
Safety. We look to the skies
for the black of the void with its billion eyes.
For the sky is the mind that grew to birth
the core and the layers and the crust of the earth.
The mind in the cavern of the skull.
The skull the limits of the skies.
The core in the dark behind the eyes.

On Not Finding the Angelry

We lower our sights and sit at the edge
of the trees and listen
and listening see
they are perched, at roost in the high branches,
infant-sized and goblin-lithe.

Some have their wings held out to dry
like sea witches;
coos and calls
ring out like notes from whittled flutes
amplified in the woods' acoustic.

Every so often, a small commotion
shakes the peace:
an Earhart or Icarus
crashes softly through the canopy,
settles safe on a platform nest –

a crown of sticks – and folds its wings,
hunkers down,
hugs its chest
and shuts its amber lantern eyes
the better to rest itself for the night.

Or one breaks out like a dove from a top hat
or a shout
or a panicked thought
and is gone. It might have never been.
We close our scopes and start for home.

Car Wash

This business of driving
reminds us of our fathers.
The low purr of fifth gear,
the sharp fumes, the biscuity
interior – has brought them,
ever-absent, nearer.
And has brought us, two
women in our thirties,
to this strange pass,
a car wash in Belfast;
where we've puzzled
and opted for 'Executive
Service' (meaning
detergent) and have minded
the instructions to wind up
our windows and sit
tight when the red light
shows, and find ourselves
delighted by a wholly
unexpected privacy
of soap suds pouring, no,
cascading in velvety waves.

And when spinning blue brushes
of implausible dimensions
are approaching the vehicle
from all directions,
what can we do
but engage in a kiss
in a world where to do so
can still stop the traffic.

And then to the rinse,
and in view once again
of incurious motorists
idling on the forecourt,
we are polished and finished
and (following instructions)
start the ignition (which
reminds us of our fathers)
and get into gear
and we're off
at the green light.

The Hopes

They extend above the houses
like mechanical giraffes.

Dignified,
they are there for a reason.

Cables hang
from their heads like harnesses.

Behind them, the sky is unusually
blue and clear

for a month so late
in the year. Don't give up.

Nature Walk

If only my bag had been large enough,
I would have brought the lonely men in parked cars
by the river. I would have brought the woman
dabbing kohl tears with the heel
of her hand. I might have brought the ancient couple
who read each word on the YOU ARE HERE
board, then turned and ambled on, heads
a little upward-tilted, showing
an interest in everything.

I would have brought the coping stone
from the twelfth pier of the original bridge, and the 4:06
from elsewhere, curving (glittering) carefully across.
And all the busy people on it; all their coats
and phones and wallets. I might
have brought the restless gulls that dropped
like paper boats on to the water. And the burger van,
the girl inside with greasy hair,
her quite unsolvable crossword.

And put them all on my nature table,
and fashioned little cardboard signs:
a small display that would speak in a way
about loneliness and life spans, parked cars and rivers.

I brought some bark, and a couple of conkers,
one still half-encased in its skin like an eye.

Self-portrait in a Broken Wing-mirror

The lens has popped from its case,
minutely cracked and yet intact, tilted
where it stopped against a rock on the tarmac.
And this could be Selkirk, washed up on a beach,
in prone position surveying the sweep
of his future sanctuary, or prison.

But no, that's me, a cubist depiction: my ear,
its swirl and ridge of pearly cartilage,
peachy lobe and indent of a piercing
not jewelled for years. I punctured that
with a nerve of steel at fifteen in a bolted
room. It was Hallowe'en. I had no fear.

The ear is parted neatly from the head
by breaks in the glass, a weird mosaic
or logic puzzle for the brain to fix.
The eyebrow, stepped in sections, stops
then starts again, recognisably mine.
The nose, at an intersection of cracks,

is all but lost except for the small sculpted
cave of a shadowy nostril. The eye
is locked on itself, the never-easy gaze
of the portraitist, the hood half open,
the hub of the pupil encircled with green
and a ring of flame. I have make-up on,

a smudging of pencil, brushed black lashes.
I'd swear the face looks younger than before,
the skin sheer, the fine wires of laughter
disappeared without the animation.
The lips are slack, pink, segmented;
a slight gravitational pull towards the earth

gives the upper one a sort of Elvis curl.
The same effect has made the cheek more full.
I have never been so still. A beautiful day
and not another car for what seems like hours.
Also in the glass, bisected, out of focus,
a streamer of road and a third of sky.

Presently, I will attempt to move,
attempt to arise in a shower of diamonds,
but first I must finish this childish contest
where one must stare the other out, not look
away, like a painting in a gallery, where
only the blink of an eye might restart time.

The Poetry Bug

is a moon-pale, lumpish creature
parcelled in translucent skin
papery as filo pastry
patterned faint as a fingerprint
is quite without face or feature
ear or eye or snout
has eight root-like
tentacles or feelers, rough
like knuckly tusks of ginger
clustered at the front.

Invisible to the naked eye
monstrous in microscopy
it loves the lovers' bed or couch
pillow, quilt or duvet
and feeds, *thrives* I should say
on human scurf and dander
indeed, is never happier
than feasting on the dust
of love's shucked husk
the micro-detritus of us.

Next Year's Luck

Next year's luck (now we're seeking it)
clings on stubborn to the upper limbs.

We reach, as children might for snow.
It is orange, crumpled, red, gold

and the unpindownable colours of flames
(new luck always manifests as old)

it is shrivelled, tindery, crisp and so
so delicate that touch might destroy it.

We have walked three seasons to be here
to watch it fall like tongues of fire

but next year's luck is taking its time
floating, meandering into our lives,

uncatchable; then sticking to our boots
and decomposing, nourishing the roots.

The Residents

Opening the door requires the breaking of a web
then spores of something in the air jab
at your throat. Your cough disturbs
an absence shaped to the room's contours.
You walk to a window silvered with a mist
that might be the breath of a captive ghost
and open the catch, admitting a gust
that rouses the papers, raises the dust.

Bunker, funk-hole, new-place-to-dwell,
the mould is blossoming on the wall.

A column of ants advancing on the carpet
swerves to avoid a rodent pellet.
An ancient terminal squats on the desk
resolutely incompatible with current systems.
Shyly, you occupy the swivel chair
which sinks by inches, open a drawer
where her pens collected year upon year
with brown coins, fluff, and hair.

Bunker, funk-hole, new-place-to-dwell,
the mould is blossoming on the wall.

You have entered the mind of the previous incumbent,
chaos, yes, but rationally governed
by a certain Havisham imperative.
You have come, like her, to 'be creative'
and 'encourage creativity', for your sins.
The radiator fills with clunks and groans.
Is this a crime-scene? Is it a shrine?
You check the phone for an outside line.

Bunker, funk-hole, new-place-to-dwell,
the mould is blossoming on the wall.

If asked, you could offer a team from forensics:
    various punched-out blister packs
    a fingerprint in a lip-gloss compact
    a half-smoked menthol cigarette
    a woollen scarf unravelling on a hook
    a mildewed draft of her second book
    a culture thriving in her unwashed cup
    a single plimsoll, size five, lace-up

and posit a case of spontaneous combustion
perhaps, or extraterrestrial abduction...
But the thought stalls, skips three years
to a bright young novelist opening the door;
the inaudible snap of a spider's thread
as he takes his first step into your head.

Bunker, funk-hole, new-place-to-dwell,
the mould is blossoming on the wall.

Self-portrait in the Dark (with Cigarette)

To sleep, perchance
to dream? No chance:
it's 4 a.m. and I'm wakeful
as an animal,
caught between your presence and the lack.
This is the realm insomniac.
On the window seat, I light a cigarette
from a slim flame and monitor the street –
a stilled film, bathed in amber,
softened now in the wake of a downpour.

Beyond the daffodils
on Magdalen Green, there's one slow vehicle
pushing its beam along Riverside Drive,
a sign of life;
and two months on
from 'moving on'
your car, that you haven't yet picked up,
waits, spattered in raindrops like bubble wrap.
Here, I could easily go off
on a riff

on how cars, like pets, look a little like their owners
but I won't 'go there',
as they say in America,
given it's a clapped-out Nissan Micra...
And you don't need to know that
I've been driving it illegally at night
in the lamp-lit silence of this city
– you'd only worry –
or, worse, that Morrissey
is jammed in the tape deck now and for eternity;

no. It's fine, all gleaming hubcaps,
seats like an upright, silhouetted couple;
from the dashboard, the wink
of that small red light I think
is a built-in security system.
In a poem
it could represent a heartbeat or a pulse.
Or loneliness: its vigilance.
Or simply the lighthouse-regular spark
of someone, somewhere, smoking in the dark.

Finisterre

Nothing to do in this place
but turn and return, or stop
and look out into nothing;
ocean and sky in a blue
confusion, the curved shriek
of a gull.

      Nothing to catch
the wind but a tourist's hair,
her summer linens blown,
her palm to the granite
cross, a squint smile
for a husband's camera flash.

         *

Sun, after days of loose
Galician rain, is siphoning
moisture from the stone
of the afternoon, while shadows
creep by increments
from under the flowers,
their little hoods and bells
frail, incongruous in the rocks.

         *

Just visible, at the foot
of the cliffs, a tiny vessel,
stopped, at anchor; a thin
figure lowering lines
and basket traps to the depths.

The great lamp sleeps my heart
my heart is contracting
after light. Aloneness
is the word I was looking for.

Belfast Waking, 6 a.m.

A maintenance man
in a small white van attends
to the city's empty confessionals,
wipes glass walls and pincers litter
(the crisp polystyrene casing
of a burger) like evidence
of the utmost significance,

wrinkles his nose at the tang of urine,
furrows his brow at a broken syringe
then finally turns to the stoical machine,

the dangling receiver's plaintive refrain
please replace the handset
and try again,

unclogs the coin-choked gullet with a tool
and a little force
like a shoulder to a wheel
or an act of necessary violence.

Sites of anonymous threat
or sanctuary, they are out of place
in the cool new century,
but he likes the way

they continue to protect
their odd rectangular blocks of light
whether the people visit them or not.

Above his head, everything is changing;
black diluting
into the blue of a morning's
infinitely slow expression.

The gradual realisation of a steeple, a ripple
of birdsong on the surface of the dawn,
a dawn that is breaking its heart over Belfast.

Béal Feirste. Red-brick terraces. Tightrope wires
and telegraph poles. The liquid slink
of a feline or a fox, one gutter
to the other, then under a fence.

A refuse vehicle's cavernous jaw
reverses massively out of an avenue,
its amber, interrupted beam
glancing hatchbacks stationed in a line.

Footsteps nearing, footsteps fading.
An upturned collar, the clearing of a throat.
A muffled *whump* as a car door shuts.
Its smooth ignition.

The moment, precise,
when the streetlamps of Belfast
quietly go out, a unanimous decision,
and the windowpanes start filling up with sky
at the advent of the ordinary
business of the day.

Once

Some words you may use only once.
Repeat them to some newer heart
*and all your accuracy is gone.**

Sweetheart, Darling. Years on,
how the old terms fail;
words that we loved with, once.

Older, on our second chance,
we stand, faltering hearts
in hands, inaccurate

and passionate, in love's
late, unfurnished rooms,
full of the words we cannot use;

and drive home, the same
streets, drop through the gears
to steer around the gone

words, the known
words, the beautiful outworn
words, those we may use only once,
all our accuracy gone.

* The lines in italics are from Denise Riley's poem 'Two Ambitions to Remember'.

Espresso

A minuscule bird
clinging to a twig

is shredding a loop
of knotted string

to a fibre-fuzzy
mist in its bill,

a haze as soft
as cotton wool

with which to line
a nest no bigger

than this small cup
I lift to my lips

while I wait for you
in this little coffee shop

on the avenue,
for such is April.

Notes Towards a Portrait of the Lobster

He is blue for the copper in his blood.
In fact, he is a length of copper pipe, or rusted pipe,
a murder weapon. A murder weapon in a game
of Cluedo, *Dalí* Cluedo. Is he a phone?

Behold the heavily calcified armour:

like any warrior, he likes to take it off
and preen in front of a full-length mirror.
He is shedding his dark blue crust
like the soft unshelling of an egg under water.

Inky eyes protrude on nubs.
Long antennae taper like whips.
He advances across the ocean floor
on eight surprisingly dainty appendages.

His frontmost chelae are enormous cutlery:
one is for crushing, the other for cutting.
If you lift him, gingerly, under the limbs
and tilt him forwards,

the weight of his claws will render them
practically useless in the air.
They will hang like concrete boxing gloves
while the creature may be closely observed.

When the lobster retreats, he will lunge
backwards with a curling and uncurling
of the abdomen, known, in the business,
as the *caridoid escape reaction*.

Note the fanned, fringed tail.

When the female moults to a soft-shelled
interim, she becomes receptive
to him, the male. When she carries
her bright blue eggs on her pleopods,

she is said to be *berried*.
There are thousands of eggs.
Little is known of the young. It is thought
that they burrow down into fine mud.

Hermit Crab

When all is tranquil,
mirror-level,
and the tremors from the sirens
of terrible gulls
have quelled, only then
does she venture from her shell,
only then one limb
from the keyhole — a tester —
is followed by others,
gradual as fingers
from a sleeve.

Then eyes
(aloft on stalks!)
and thread antennae
dowsing for signs,
tensed as reins,
sensate, curious.
Come out, Pagurus.
Pagurus Bernhardus.

Miniature
charioteer
in the field of
her life, she hauls
her nook behind her,
rounds on a topshell
larger than her own
(in fact, a beauty),
stops to inspect it,

turning it over,
inserting a leg
like a pipe-cleaner
into the pearl-
smooth chamber.

Chosen? Yes.
She readies herself
then eases her mass
like a cork from a bottle,
plugs in fast
to her new abode
with a twist to fit it,
a hook in the whirl,
secure. Snug
as an earplug in an ear.

Desiccation,
predation,
abrasion on the rocks…
Her daily prayer:
the perils of the shoreline.
Quick, retreat!
She draws in tight
to her porcelain cell,
claws up front
like a boxer's
peek-a-boo
behind his gloves.

Hiddenness
is the default policy.
A low profile, a bent
for privacy. Only
the lucky and
the fighters survive.
Come out, Pagurus.
Pagurus Bernhardus.

White

I stepped from my skis and stumbled in, like childhood,
knee deep, waist deep, chest deep, falling
for the sake of being caught
in its grip.

It was crisp and strangely dry and I thought: I could drop
here and sleep in my own shape, happily,
as the hare fits
to its form.

I could lie undiscovered like a fossil in a rock
until a hammer's gentle knock might
split it open; warm
and safe

in a wordless place (the snowfall's ample increase),
and finally drift into the dream of white
from which there is no
way back.

I placed myself in that cold case like an instrument into velvet
and slept.

Derry

I was born between the Creggan and the Bogside
    to the sounds of crowds and smashing glass,
by the River Foyle with its suicides and rip tides.
    I thought that city was nothing less

than the whole and rain-domed universe.
    A teacher's daughter, I was one of nine
faces afloat in the looking-glass
    fixed in the hall, but which was mine?

I wasn't ever sure.
    We walked to school, linked hand in hand
in twos and threes like paper dolls.
    I slowly grew to understand

the way the grey Cathedral cast
    its shadow on our learning, cool,
as sunlight crept from east to west.
    The adult world had tumbled into hell

from where it wouldn't find its way
    for thirty years. The local priest
played Elvis tunes and made us pray
    for starving children, and for peace,

and lastly for 'The King'. At mass we'd chant
    hypnotically, *Hail Holy Queen,*
mother of mercy; sing to Saint
    Columba of his *Small oak grove, O Derry mine.*

*

We'd cross the border in our red Cortina,
    stopped at the checkpoint just too long
for fractious children, searched by a teenager
    drowned in a uniform, cumbered with a gun,

who seemed to think we were trouble-on-the-run
    and not the Von Trapp family singers
harmonizing every song
    in rounds to pass the journey quicker.

Smoke coiled up from terraces
    and fog meandered softly down the valley
to the Brandywell and the greyhound races,
    the ancient walls with their huge graffiti,

arms that encircled the old city
    solidly. Beyond their pale,
the Rossville flats, mad vision of modernity;
    snarling crossbreeds leashed to rails.

A robot under remote control like us
    commenced its slow acceleration
towards a device at number six,
    home of the moderate politician;

only a hoax, for once, some boys
    had made from parcel tape and batteries
gathered on forays to the BSR,
    the disused electronics factory.

*

The year was nineteen eighty-one,
    the reign of Thatcher. 'Under Pressure'
was the song that played from pub to pub
    where talk was all of hunger strikers

in the Maze, our jail within a jail.
    A billboard near Free Derry Corner
clocked the days to the funerals
    as riots blazed in the city centre.

Each day, we left for the grammar school,
    behaved ourselves, pulled up our socks
for benevolent Sister Emmanuel
    and the Order of Mercy. Then we'd flock

to the fleet of buses that ferried us
    back to our lives, the Guildhall Square
where Shena Burns our scapegoat drunk
    swayed in her chains like a dancing bear.

On the couch, we cheered as an Irish man
    bid for the Worldwide Featherweight title
and I saw blue bruises on my mother's arms
    when her sleeve fell back while filling the kettle

for tea. My bed against the door,
    I pushed the music up as loud
as it would go and curled up on the floor
    to shut the angry voices out.

*

My candle flame faltered in a cup;
    we were stood outside the barracks in a line
chanting in rhythm, calling for a stop
    to strip searches for the Armagh women.

The proof that Jesus was a Derry man?
    Thirty-three, unemployed and living with his mother,
the old joke ran. While half the town
    were queuing at the broo, the fortunate others

bent to the task of typing out the cheques.
    Boom! We'd jump at another explosion,
windows buckling in their frames, and next
    you could view the smouldering omission

in a row of shops, the missing tooth
    in a street. Gerry Adams' mouth
was out of sync in the goldfish bowl
    of the TV screen, our dubious link

with the world. Each summer, one by one,
    my sisters upped and crossed the water,
armed with a grant from the government
    – the Butler system's final flowers –

until my own turn came about:
    I watched that place grow small before
the plane ascended through the cloud
    and I could not see it clearly any more.

Re-entering the Egg

Like some magnificent Swiss clock,
the house has been rebuilt
in the same position, in that Georgian street.
Tall and lean, it tilts towards us,
lists like a ship on rough seas
as it always did, only look (how clever!)
the front can be opened
with this small lever.

A tiny family fills the rooms.
In one, a wife is breathing fire,
genies whirling in the air.
In one, we hear the Strong Man's snores
rumbling under a mound of clothes
like a subterranean train.
In one, first floor, a spangled girl
enters in her diary: *I am headed for a fall.*
In one, girl-twins, conjoined
at the skull, freak themselves
to a pitch of shrieks, *A rat, I saw it! There!*
In one, a mermaid, washed up on the floor,
amber-lit in the notional glow
of a three-bar fire, strums a guitar,
hooks blonde hair behind one ear.
Like a baby bird re-entering the egg,
the smallest girl's soft breath
knits round her like a shell, like pearl,
where she's curled up sleeping
on the topmost bunk
of a creaking bed.

A television flickers blue
in another room
and a British voice reports the news
as smoke-rings loosen in the air, disperse,
and turfs collapse in the grate
beneath the glowing coal
in the ruptured chest
of the Sacred Heart.

Out of time, they go about their lives
unaware of our scrutiny.
Close it up. That's enough for now.

Boredoom

The world was due to end next week
according to someone whose brother
had read Nostradamus. Magpies,
two for joy. Walk round ladders, *quick*,

touch wood. We mimed the prayer
of the Green Cross Code and waited,
good, at the side of the road. Blessed
ourselves when the ambulance sailed

by on a blue (our fingers, toes). Lay
awake in the fret of the night, thinking
about the Secret of Fatima, the four-
minute warning, the soft-boiled egg.

Our boomerang did not come back.
Frisbees lodged in the canopies
of trees forever, turning black.
I poked out moss from paving slabs

half-dreamingly, with an ice-pop stick,
then leapt at the looped rope of my name
called from a yard and dawdled home
trailing a strange tune on the xylophone railings.

The future lived in the crystal ball
of a snake preserved in alcohol
in my grandmother's attic. I looked,
on tiptoe, out through the lens

of the highest window; learned
the silver river's turn, the slogans daubed
on the ancient walls, the column of smoke
where something always burned.

The theatrical death of my maternal grandmother as revealed in a 1960s glitter globe

I give it a shake and look
again and spot
a pair of bunioned shoes
beneath a portly lady
at a table, contemplating
soup. The conversation
batted to and fro
with my mother
through the scullery door
concerns the première
'on Broadway!' of
Philadelphia, Here I Come!
Before the lights
go out and she hits
the boards, and a slow day
falters for a moment –
'Isn't it great,' she shouts,
'to see a Derry man
getting on?'

Heritance

From her? Resilience. Generosity.
A teacher's gravitas.
Irish stew. A sense
of the ridiculous. High ceilings.
Neither a borrower nor a lender be.
Operatic plotlines.
Privacy.

An artery leading to the Spanish Armada,
a galleon dashed on the rocks at Moville, a sunken
grave, *se llama Hernando,*
black hair, despair,
a rose between the teeth.
Bullets. Books.
A low-toned voice.

An Antarctic explorer in a fur-lined hood
with the face of a pugilist
and a Russian wife in Brooklyn.
Bottles, half-full,
tilting in the ottoman.
O rhesus negative.
Tact, to a point.

Uncle Joe walking out of the Dáil in '22,
sold down the river.
An historical anger.
Stand-up piano.
Pilgrim feet.
A comic turn of phrase.
An iron constitution.

The Analyst's Couch

I was not there when the soldier was shot, so I didn't see him
carried up the street and manoeuvred
through our propped front door.
Who took his weight, the women or the soldiers?
Blood, seeping into the cushions, dark brown stuff
like HP sauce, soaking thoroughly into the foam, the worn
upholstery of the enemy. *Laid out on the sofa
of eternity*, its faded tweed, its sag, its hoard
of household smells, fluff and pens, small change
and lost buttons. *Am I making this up?* Its animalness.
Paw-footed, it pads from the room, the soldier lying bleeding on its back.
No it doesn't.

Helicopters

Over time, you picture them
after dark, in searches

focusing on streets and houses
close above the churches

or balancing
on narrow wands of light.

And find so much depends upon
the way you choose

to look at them:
high in the night

their minor flares confused
among the stars, there –

almost beautiful.
Or from way back

over the map
from where they might resemble

a business of flies
around the head-wound of an animal.

North to the South

1

The map unfolded in the car
like a kite, a barely
controllable thing
to be wrestled, my father
overcome.

A giant's hands
might have practised origami,
a bird, or a boat
on which an impossible dream
might stay afloat.

2

A head through the window
on the driver's side.

Where have we come from?
Where are we going?

Eight little girls and a dog
spill out.

Aunty Máire was famous
for spelling out her name

P-Ó-G M-O T-H-Ó-I-N,
which they duly wrote down.

3

You are giving the vast Atlantic
to your father, bucketful
by bucketful, padding

to and fro on the damp strand
to store it at his feet
in a hole where

it only appears to vanish.

The Search

All day we searched
for the wedding ring,
with a childish devotion
to the task. Marion,
in her post-natal sorrows
back at the house, twirling
a lock of her hair
over and over
and over, that faraway
look. *Poor Marion.*

Close to the dunes
we sifted, dug. One
patch of sand soon merged
with another. Not a land-
mark, not a post or rock,
the script of the beach
erased by weather.
Our shadows loomed
on the lit strand,
conducting their own
investigation.

A small haul of items
amassed: a conch,
a twist of fisherman's
rope, the parched sole
of a shoe. Cloudy gems
of greenish glass; a picnic
cup, some patterned
cloth. At a loss,

we'd play or bury
each other: feet,
knees, hips, chest; sand
in our hair, in our cuffs,
in the turn-ups
of our jeans, sand
in the creases of our skin,
as we scaled the heights
of the dunes and leapt
for dear life
into thin

air. Thirty years.
The coolness of that sand;
just coarse enough
to hold itself together
in the wind, but soft
like powdered gold
where our discarded
shadows had been thrown.

Magi

Joseph was the Famous Grouse,
and the Virgin Mary, the Babycham deer.
Standing in for the sheep and the ass
were the Black & White distillery terriers.

The shepherd loitering shyly with a lamp
was McEwan's Laughing Cavalier
and the followed star was a golden Harp,
the swaddling cloth a Smithwick's towel.

Up on the walls where they hung all year
were Pio, Pearse and Johnnie Walker
carrying whiskey, liberty and prayer,
gifts befitting an Irish saviour.

The Republicans

Their walls are like any other walls, muffled in layers of paste and paper.
Squares compete with a carpet's swirls. The room is a-clutter with adolescents,
children, ashtrays, dirty cups; a television's flash and jabber.

A man reclines in an armchair, dragged up close to the hearth, his feet
on the shelf. Glowing coals are banked with slack. Cooking smells waft in
from beyond the door. Two schoolgirls braid each other's hair.

Jesus opens his ruptured chest in a frame; in another, Jesus again
at an earlier age, in his mother's arms. In a third, a triptych in household gloss
depicts a map, a gun and a dove. *Ireland unfree shall never be at peace*

spelled out by sons in prison workshops. The republicans
rest their plates on their knees and gobble up their dinners, quickly.
Mince. Potatoes. Peas or beans. They light their fags and inhale, deeply.

Don't speak to the Brits, just pretend they don't exist

Two rubber bullets stand on the shelf,
from Bloody Sunday – mounted in silver,

space rockets docked and ready to go off;
like the Sky Ray Lolly that crimsons your lips

when the orange Quencher your brother gets
attracts a wasp that stings him on the tongue.

'Tongue' is what they call the Irish language,
'native tongue' you're learning at school.

Kathleen is sent home from the Gaeltacht
for speaking English, and it's there

at the Gaeltacht, ambling back
along country roads in pure darkness

that a boy from Dublin
talks his tongue right into your mouth,

holds you closely in the dark and calls it
French kissing (he says this in English).

Positions Prior to the Arrival of the Military

Mother (out for the count) has been carried
from the ring. *Ding ding!* we have a victor,

Father, who has vanished in a puff of smoke
from his pipe, to return in the small hours.

Sister has stepped from her sleeping body
and floats about unnoticed amongst us,

a dream she will later recount,
while brother, who sleeps on the ceiling

lately, gazes down like a Sistine cherub
with a lute, a stain spreading on the sheet

where he used to sleep, before
he was safe. The screen in the corner

has much to offer: heart-warming stories,
Little House on the Prairie.

Satellite beams are connecting all this
with New York, Bangkok, the Moon (in theory).

You're climbing the banisters, monkeying up
through the house without the aid of stairs –

a test, if passed successfully,
that will save the world from nuclear meltdown.

Rat-a-tat-tat at the door and the dog
is going berserk. All hesitate

Your Grandmother's House

The Toby jugs on her mantelshelf
are like a row of punters sitting at the bar,
red-cheeked, ever the worse for wear. In a mirror,
the Ulster Television News
or Scene Around Six: the latest murders.
Her call, weak, from the top of the stairs

(where is he?) *Son are you there?*, the stairs
creaking, footfalls, one by one. She steadies herself
in the unlit hall, enters and yes, she could murder
a nice cup of tea. A booth like in the bar;
a black banquette. The lilac light of the news
enfolds you in its trance, casts glints like a mirror-

ball around the room. In the convex mirror
fixed like a porthole to the wall, you stare
from far away, re-scaled, and watch the news
of a missing child as she frisks the shelf
for the spectacles she might have left in the bar
for goodness sake, but no, sure here they are. A murder

inquiry is what they want but is it a murder?
Nobody knows, with no body and the case a mirror
of the case last year (the talk of the bar)
where the child had been cowering under the stairs
all the while. She sets her saucer on the shelf
and settles back to wait for the news

headlines to repeat again. Your new
uniform prickles skin as you browse the murder
mysteries huddled fatly on a single shelf
and wait for your father to enter this mirror-
life in which he's come to live, in a room upstairs,
and take his place at the booth he calls 'the breakfast bar'

and make some awkward conversation. A bar
of chocolate. A soft drink. He'll angle for news
of your sisters, brother... *How's your mother?* You'll stare
ahead and fidget, What do *you* think? The murder
story cross-fades into the sports results and the mirror
holds a stranger, or some other self

who stares back blank as the child in the murder.
At the breakfast bar, as you knew
you would, you shelve this scene and exit the mirror.

The Brits

Whatever it was they were looking for, they liked
to arrive in the small hours, take us by surprise,
avoiding our eyes like gormless youngfellas
shuffling at a dance. My mother spoke:
a nod from the leader and the batch of heavy rifles
was stacked, *clackety-clack*, like a neat camp fire
under the arch of the hall table – her one
condition, with so many children
in their beds – each gun placed by a soldier
whose face, for an instant, hung in the mirror.
This done, the load of them thundered up the stairs,
filling our rooms like news of a tragedy.

Last night I dreamt of tiny soldiers,
like the action figures I played with as a child.
Fay Wray soldiers in the clumsy hands of Kong,
little Hasbro troopers in the massive hands of God.
I'd like to remove their camouflage and radios,
to dress them up in doll-sized clothes; little high-street shirts,
jeans, trainers, the strip of ordinary sons and brothers.
I'd like to hand them back to their mothers.

A Library Book

'Look after that, it's a library book.'
Tikki Tikki Tembo, the story of a boy
who fell down a well. The story of his brother
running to fetch the old man with the ladder.
Library books were special, hard-backed
ones that opened wide with creaks
like tomes that wizards possessed. Rest
your cheek against the cold slip-cover,
pictures vivid underneath. Run your fingertip
down the column of dates, stamped
for return by a kind librarian, each
corresponding to a child, a reader,
who carried it home to the order
or chaos of their lives and lost themselves
in the story. *Tikki tikki tembo no sa rembo*

chari bari ruchi pip peri pembo!
My sister and I could deliver his name in one breath –
a spell, or a poem by heart. Years later,
it took only one of us to start
and the words unfurled on cue
like a streamer. In student digs. By intercity
coach, I'd visit her in gas-fire flats
where she nursed the baby that arrived
before she was grown, where my sister
started falling, gradually at first,
into one particular dark. There was no
old man with a ladder, *climbing step
over step.* I go back to the book,
retrieved in an internet search, desperate
to remember what happened.

A little girl I knew when she was my mother

emerged from the pages of a bed

      from sheets the colour of old snow

crawled from the petals of the Weeping Rose

      from silks suffused with smoke

        and sweat

dragged her wings from a chrysalis

slipped from the folds of the Virgin's robes

uncurled her limbs
          like an opening fist
                  ravelled
      free of the winding cloths

felt for the floor
        with the ball of her foot

      found a swirling-patterned carpet

raised a hand to her sleep-stiff hair

      breathed the ancient bedroom air.

There were black flags hanging from the houses

      rags fluttering in the breeze.

*

Miles away, a dressing table.
Angels escort her ineffable steps

to rest on a piano stool,
all that is left of the instrument,

while under the seat, sheet music
hums to innocent childhood airs.

I see them floating in the triptych mirrors
the little girls I knew when they were my mothers.

They look down at their old hands,
jewelled rings screwed over knuckles.

There's a woman trapped in the centre of their body
that no one can remember, as if in amber.

They look down at their old hands
and cry, petals falling from their eyes.

(after Louise Bourgeois)

Signature

When I finally gave up and became my mother, I concentrated hard
and wrote myself a note for the teacher, kept
a steady hand
as I leant to the slant of her signature
in the style she had introduced to the schools of the North. I ripped
    a leaf
from her pad of Basildon Bond and found myself an envelope.
Dear Mrs Brophy... absent yesterday, because... Because
I had become my mother, the flourish
on that sloping *B*
was as natural to me as it was to my sister and co-forger who,
    ten years later,
when we dug out her flat in Morningside into black bin bags,
    after the breakdown,
had written on a card fixed in the nameplate on her door, *her name*
in that very same hand, the very same
flourish on the capital *B*, as natural to her as it was to me.

A Simple Modern Hand

1

The italic characteristics
begin to emerge:
slope,
economy of stroke.

They say compression
is the essence,
elements all
encased in the oval

n. u. v. a. o. x.
each confined
to its egg
or box. O mother,

what am I hankering after
with spidery hand,
signature pressure?
Do I mean

this tentative pen
to discover... What?
The torched
pages of a book?

Flakes of the truth
like black moths
at a grate?
A fire's cool erasure?

2

My mother's hand has been lost for good
like a maiden name, or a fingerprint
seared off by the thief who faked his own death
in a book – the buoyant cursive of her youth
with which she wrote to Alain – *amour!* –
the mythical Parisian whom all of our mothers
should really have married, but somehow let go,
to then fall prey to our no-good fathers
and all the predictable sinkers of a mother's
lot, on the sleeves, the spirit, and the heart.

3

One method of refining
a good italic hand
is by sandwiching *m*
between pairs of letters
mama – mama –
emem – emem –

denoting the bilabial
interrupted hum
with its stem and arches
and wavelike
momentum, bearing
on its shoulders
the pressure
of intention.

o is the governing shape,
the model, the oval
ever-elliptical hoop.
o is a nutshell,
Phoenician eyeball,
all-seeing, *o*
is the mouthshape
of surprise.

Extending the cross stroke
of an elegant *t*
will fluently link
to the letters that follow
ta – te – ti –
ti – toe – tum

and carry us on
to the slant
of the *h* or the shibboleth
haitch, a simple
single stroke,
alphabetically eighth

(and 'The Eighth'
incidentally,
was the title of a poem,
the only one she wrote).

e is the oval again,
the curled
most common vowel
in the English tongue,

the loop
tucked into
the centre
of the downstroke
which exits with the lift
to the terminal *r*.

From the *r*'s main stem,
the small, shoulder upstroke
should not be overdone;
if drawn too long
it may well interfere
with the letters that follow,

in this case none,
as we come to the end
of our word for today
and lift our pen
and our gaze
from where the ink
already dries.

4

With this transitional script
we mark a change.

5

We begin with a tiny corner
of a white page, edged
in bluish flame,

a fragment that increases
as the smouldering fringe expands,
paper forming in its wake,

neat lines of naïve script
– rounded letters,
circles adorning the *is* –

and the arc of flame moves on
like the widening
fingertip search of an area,

then narrows again
and peters away
revealing the newborn opposite

corner of the page,
an unburned sheet of paper.
Is it a letter? What does it say?

Wait, it is the first-burnt leaf
of a book, page 1, which now
takes its place on top

of the re-formed volume,
which slips into its cover
and is bound, for words

are indeed binding
(the reason for the burning
before all this),

and thus we return the word
to the world, and thus
we replace the heart

into the hearth
as we place the book
back into the hands

of its owner, only a child, a girl,
who smiles at us
and leans to her writing.

Mammy Dozes

Mammy dozes in her chair.
Cushions packed in soft layers
are glowing with her heat.
Eighty years have lent her skin

a bruised look in composure,
a touch of purples
to the hollows, so Mammy dozing
resembles a boxer in defeat.

She could be anyone's mother,
any one of the old, alone
in living rooms throughout
this town, prey to junk mail,

meter readers, window cleaners,
priests. On *Deal or No Deal*
someone is winning, pounds
clocking up on screen.

In a peaceful corner of the
universe, with bulky silver cars
in drives, magpies flashing
on the roof, Mammy sleeps.

Pisces

When the tide withdraws
like a jeweller's cloth
to reveal a mile
of glittering rocks,

what's not to love?
What's to stop
a human like you
in coat and gumboots

clambering out
to the furthest reach,
as near as dammit
to the sea floor?

What's to prevent
a human like you
from choosing a spot
on the planetary rocks

to live,
resolute as a limpet
sits tight
in its home scar?

The hermit crab
in its hermit shell.
You in your skull,
your pulsing fontanelle,

the North Sea
creeping up on you
again, fingertip
by fingertip, ready

to pounce

Asylum

(Iona)

Should a guest blow in from the north of Ireland,
    buffeted by the wind,

should the shadow of a cross, afloat on the water,
    mirror the flight of a pilgrim guest

pitching an effortful course through the buffeting gusts,
    this far from the north of Ireland;

should the pilgrim guest, whittled with hunger, depleted
    in reserves, lose altitude

and collapse on the stones of your own small island,
    beaten and worn,

stagger on the shingle, dragging magnificent wings like a cape,
    like an airman trailing his billowing silks,

you must lift this creature and carry it, gathered
    in your arms, over the field to the bothy,

and there, attend to its invalid needs
    for three consecutive days and nights,

during which time it may huddle in a corner, throat retracted
    into its ruff, stern as a cleric, gimlet-eyed,

yet gulping the silver herrings you proffer
    like pills, gaining strength, getting well,

till you walk with it back to the narrow beach, on day four,
    watch it take a run

and lift with the gawkiest of take-offs, creaking beats
    of its great span, neck and bill extended like an arrow

pointing the route to my old homeland
    — which is why I am so solicitous of your kindness —

ruling a line straight south to Malin Head
    and home, the sweet district of Ireland.

After Adomnán's account of St Columba's prophecy of the heron

Index of Titles